Side by Side

How can we learn
and work well together?

page 4

Literature

Related Readings and Projects

page 28

Lemonade Stand

by Myra Cohn Livingston

Every summer
under the shade
we fix up a stand
to sell lemonade.

A stack of cups,
a pitcher of ice,
a shirtboard sign
to tell the price.

A dime for the big,
A nickel for small.
The nickel cup's short.
The dime cup's tall.

Plenty of sugar
to make it sweet,
and sometimes cookies
for us to eat.

But when the sun
moves into the shade
it gets too hot
to sell lemonade.

Nobody stops
so we put things away
and drink what's left
and start to play.

Lemonade
small cup 5¢
big cup 10¢

Let's Work Together

The children in "Lemonade Stand" are working together to make money. They are also selling cool lemonade to neighbors on a hot day. People work together in many ways to make their neighborhoods nice. What could you do to make your neighborhood a nice place to live?

Collect Facts and Ideas

1 Find out what people do to make your neighborhood or a friend or relative's neighborhood a nice place to live.

2 Find out what else could be done in your neighborhood to make it a nice place to live. Ask people who work in your neighborhood. Tally their answers.

Put It All Together

3 Make a list of good things that are being done in your neighborhood or in a friend or relative's neighborhood. List new things that could be done. Look at your tally marks. Make a graph of people's answers.

Prepare and Share

4 Choose something from your graph or list that you would like to do for your neighborhood.

5 Make a plan that tells how you could help. Make a poster that tells about your plan. Share it with your classmates.

Tortoise Brings the Mail

by Dee Lillegard

illustrated by Jillian Lund

Way out in the countryside, there lived a tortoise whose job was to carry the mail.

Tortoise loved his job. He put all the mail in all the right boxes, and he was nice and friendly. But everybody thought he was too slow.

One day Crow said, "I can do better than Tortoise. I can fly in a straight line. I can go fast."

Everybody else said, "Let's let Crow bring our mail."

Tortoise had to agree. "Delivering the mail is very important. Let the very best one do it."

So Crow got the job that Tortoise loved.

Poor Tortoise. I may as well just lie in the sun and snooze, he said to himself. But after a while . . .

A letter came floating down out of the air and landed on Tortoise's nose.

"My goodness," he said. "I'd better help Crow deliver this letter."

Then another letter drifted down, and another, for Crow was dropping the mail as he flew.

Letters landed on treetops and rooftops, and in places nobody could reach. There was a big fuss all over the countryside.

"Nobody appreciates me," said Crow. "I quit." And he flew away home with his feathers ruffled.

Tortoise was so happy to have his old job back. He hummed and smiled to himself. Until . . .

Rabbit said, "I can do better than Tortoise and Crow. I can run fast. And I will put the mail in the mailboxes."

Everybody else said, "Let's let Rabbit bring our mail."

Tortoise had to agree. "Delivering the mail is very important. Let the very best one do it."

So Rabbit got the job that Tortoise loved.

Poor Tortoise. He lay in the sun and snoozed until . . . loud shouts woke him.

"This isn't my letter!"

"This isn't my package!"

It seems that Rabbit had gone racing through bushes and hopping over logs. She had put everything in the mailboxes. But . . .

Rabbit ran so fast, she did not have time to read names. She put all the letters and packages in the wrong mailboxes.

TO:
ELI ELK
PONDEROSA
PATH
MEADOW #1

CAMERON CATERPILLAR

PENELOPE PORCUPINE
OH MY MEADOW

HEY!
Benjamin Bat CAVE #2
ROCKY RIDGE

"My goodness," said Tortoise, "I'd better help Rabbit learn who's who."

There was a big fuss all over the countryside. Rabbit stopped in her tracks.

"Nobody appreciates me," she said. "I quit." And she dragged herself home, all tuckered out.

Tortoise went all over the countryside, taking the mail from the wrong boxes and putting it in the right ones. It took him half the evening.

But Tortoise was so happy to have his old job back. He hummed and smiled to himself. Until . . .

Fox said, "I can do better than Tortoise and Crow and Rabbit. I'm fast and I'm smart. And I never make mistakes."

Everybody else said, "Let's let Fox bring our mail."

Again Tortoise had to agree. "Delivering the mail is very important. Let the very best one do it."

So Fox got the job that Tortoise loved. Fox was not very friendly. But he whizzed through the bushes. He leaped over logs. He read each name and put every piece of mail into the right box.

Well, *almost* every piece of mail . . .

You see, Fox sniffed everything first. And when he smelled a package he liked, he kept it for himself. Nobody fussed about this. They had no idea what Fox was up to. They thought he was doing a great job.

Poor Tortoise. He was getting very tired of lying in the sun. "I think I will take a walk," he said one Sunday morning.

Tortoise walked along his old mail route until he came to Fox's house.

"Fox should be home today," said Tortoise. "I will stop and congratulate him on the great job he is doing."

Tortoise knocked on Fox's door. But there was no answer. Tortoise knocked again and then stepped inside. To his surprise, Tortoise saw all the packages that Fox had kept for himself.

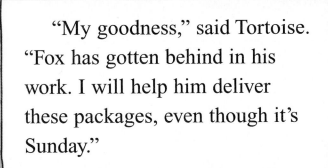

"My goodness," said Tortoise. "Fox has gotten behind in his work. I will help him deliver these packages, even though it's Sunday."

So Tortoise took the packages and began to deliver them. It took him all day and half the evening.

"But why didn't Fox bring us our packages?" everybody asked Tortoise when they saw him.

"Delivering the mail is a big job," said Tortoise.

He was happy to be helping Fox. And he was happy to be doing his old job.

When Fox came home and saw that all his treasures were gone, he was furious!

"Everything is gone!" Fox shouted.

Just then, Tortoise stopped by on his way back.

"Don't worry, Fox," he said. "I delivered the packages for you."

Fox took a deep breath and smiled a toothy smile. "Thank you, my friend," he said.

"You're very welcome," said Tortoise. "I want to congratulate you on the great job you're doing."

"How very nice of you," said Fox.

Clever Tortoise, Fox thought. He has outfoxed me. He knows I meant to keep those packages. But he is much too clever to say so. That night Fox packed his bags and left the forest forever.

The next day, Tortoise was surprised to learn that Fox was gone.

He was even more surprised when, all over the countryside, everybody else said, "From now on, Tortoise, we want you to bring our mail. Now we know, you are the very best one."

Tortoise beamed. "My goodness," he said. "I'd better get busy."

Then off he went to deliver the mail. He hummed and smiled to himself—for Tortoise loved his job!

Book

Animal Fantasy

Tortoise Brings the Mail is about a tortoise who can read and deliver the mail. He can do things that real animals cannot do. All the animals in the story can do things that people do. They all have mailboxes and houses. They can even talk to each other! When animals in a story act like people, the story is called an animal fantasy.

Think of other animal fantasies. What do the story animals do that real animals cannot do?

Find Animal Fantasies

Look for animal fantasies in the library. Think about these questions:

- Can the animals talk?
- Do the animals wear clothes?
- Do the animals have feelings?

Here are some animal fantasies you might find:

Miss Spider's New Car

Toot & Puddle

To Annabella Pelican *from* **Thomas Hippopotamus**

Fair

Think and Read

1. Read animal fantasies. Make a list of what the animals do and think. Make a list of how they act. Write the titles of the animal fantasy books you read.

2. Make up an animal character that is like some of the characters you have read. Draw a picture on a large sheet of paper.

3. Use your list to write words that describe your character.

Share

4. Share your drawing with your class. Tell how your character is like some of the characters you have read about. Tell why your animal character could not be a real animal.

Building an Igloo

**written and photographed
by Ulli Steltzer**

Winter in the Northern Arctic is long and cold. A
new layer of white snow covers land and sea every
day, packing down hard in some places and settling
loosely in others.

Trees have never grown in this part of the world.
For hundreds of years the Inuit people of the Northern
Arctic built winter houses of snow called igloos. Snow
was everywhere, and the only tool needed was a knife
made of bone, antler, or walrus tusk.

Tookillkee Kiguktak lives in Canada, on Ellesmere Island. He does not live in an igloo; like all the Inuit of today, he lives in a house. But when Tookillkee was a little child he lived in an igloo, and when he was a boy he learned how to build one. Ever since, when he goes hunting far away for a musk ox or a polar bear, he builds an igloo for shelter.

A hunter never goes alone on a long trip. Tookillkee likes to take along Jopee, one of his four sons. Of course Jopee—like his father—long ago learned how to build an igloo.

It takes several hours of hard work to build a good igloo. The most important thing is to find the right kind of snow. Not too soft, not too hard.

Tookillkee starts walking over the land. With his carpenter saw he checks how deep and good the snow is. Once he has found a large area of the right kind of snow, he makes a circle in the snow with his feet. This is where he will build his igloo.

Tookillkee outlines the blocks in the snow before he cuts them. Then, with the blade of the saw, he lifts up each one. A block can weigh from eighteen to twenty-seven pounds, depending on its size.

When he has cut all the blocks, it is time to start building the igloo.

He cuts diagonally into the blocks to start a spiral.

Jopee helps with the carrying. Before bringing a fresh block, he waits until his father has set the last one in position.

After setting each block, Tookillkee trims and cleans its surface with a long knife.

The final blocks that round off the top need to be carefully shaped and fit.

Tookillkee reaches up and places the last block. He is locked in.

With his knife, he cuts a low doorway and crawls out.

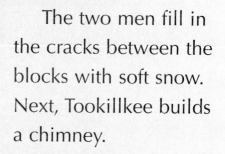

The two men fill in the cracks between the blocks with soft snow. Next, Tookillkee builds a chimney.

Then he cuts a window in the front, above the entrance. He has chosen a piece of ice from the ocean for a windowpane. It allows light to reach the inside, a strange blue-green light like that surrounding a swimmer underwater.

Tookillkee decides to build a porch. It will keep the cold air from coming inside and will give him storage space, especially for food, boots, and bulky clothing. He cuts more snow blocks, attaches them to both sides of the igloo's entrance, and rounds off the top.

The igloo is ready.

It is evening. Father and son settle down inside. Tomorrow will be a day of hunting.

Step by Step

In "Building an Igloo" the author tells how to build an igloo. The author gives important details so the directions are clear. He also uses words such as *start*, *before*, *after*, *next* and *then*. The words help the reader follow the steps in order. How do these words help you understand how the igloo is built?

You can write your own directions telling how to make or do something. Think of something that you know how to make—an art project, a model, a special sandwich, or even a play fort! Write step-by-step directions for someone to make the same thing. As you write, remember to:

- Tell one step at a time.
- Put the steps in order.
- Use words such as *first*, *next*, and *last* to help readers follow your directions.
- Give details to make the steps clear.

Draw a picture to go with your directions. Then read them to a classmate. Ask if you need to add more information.

Step 5

Step 4

Step 3

Step 2

Step 1

All Kinds of Homes

Native Americans in the Arctic learned to use ice to build igloos. The igloos were used as shelter. Shelter is something that covers or protects you from weather or danger.

Air holes allow air to move in and out.

The roof of the igloo traps warm air inside.

Cold air falls into a cold sink and flows outside.

Long ago Native Americans lived all over the United States. Native Americans built homes to shelter themselves from weather and protect themselves from danger. When they needed shelter, they used what was around them. How do you think Native Americans who lived in the desert built their homes? Some Native Americans lived in a forest. What kind of homes do you think they built?

Look at the pictures. How did different Native American groups build their homes? What did they use to make these homes? How did their homes protect them from weather and danger?

a chickee in the Southeast

tepees in the Plains

a longhouse in the Northeast

a plank house in the Northwest

Look in books about Native Americans. Use a map to find where Native American groups lived. Draw pictures of the homes they built. Put them on the map. Use materials in your classroom to build a model of one of these homes.

an adobe village in the Southwest

Incredible Ice

The island where Tookillkee lives is so far north that ice covers the land and the ocean most of the time. Snow falls month after month. Slowly, it piles up and gets heavy. After many years, the snow forms huge amounts of ice. These icy forms are called *glaciers*.

Glaciers seem solid like rock. They seem very still. But every day, glaciers move. They creep very, very slowly down toward the sea. They cut through the rock and earth and change the land.

Sometimes a part of a glacier that is near the sea breaks off. The breaking makes strange, loud sounds. The part that comes off is called an iceberg.

Icebergs are beautiful. They are bright white and can have interesting shapes. But icebergs are dangerous too. That is because the part you see is only a small part of the whole iceberg. Ships that get too close to an iceberg may crash against the part that is hidden underwater and sink.

Find out more about ice.
Try one or more of
these ideas.

What You Need
3 clear plastic cups
ice cubes
a permanent marker
a scale for weighing in
   grams or ounces
a freezer

What You Do

1 *How is ice different
from water?*
Pour water in a cup. Draw a
line to show the top of the
water. Weigh the water. Then
put the cup in the freezer.
After the water is frozen,
draw a line to show the
top of the ice. What
happened to the water
when it turned to ice?

2 *What happens
when water freezes?*
Weigh the cup of ice.
Write the weight.
Compare the weight of
the ice to the weight of
the water. Are they the
same?

3 *What does a floating ice
cube do?*
Put some water in another
cup. Drop an ice cube in the
water. How much of the ice
can you see above the
water? Draw a picture
of what you see.

Reader Response

Think About a Question

1 How can we learn and work well together? In *Tortoise Brings the Mail*, the animals learn a lesson about work. In "Building an Igloo" Tookillkee and his son work together to build an igloo. What do you know about working nicely with others? Make a poster that tells people how to work together.

Ask a Question

2 When Tookillkee was a child, he lived in an igloo. List three questions you would like to ask Tookillkee about living in an igloo.

Use New Words

3 In "Building an Igloo" you learned some new words. List five new words about building an igloo. Write why they are important.

Connect What You Read

4 The animals learn a lesson in *Tortoise Brings the Mail*. Can you think of another story where characters learn a lesson? Write the title of the story and the lesson the characters learn.

Take a Careful Look

5 If Tortoise were to go out of town, what advice do you think he would give the animals about delivering the mail? Write your answer.